10/22

THE PRACTICE OF THE PRESENCE OF GOD

The Practice of the Presence of God

Brother Lawrence

Edited and Paraphrased by
Donald E. Demaray

ALBA·HOUSE   alba house   NEW·YORK

SOCIETY OF ST. PAUL, 2187 VICTORY BLVD., STATEN ISLAND, NEW YORK 10314

ST PAULS

Library of Congress Cataloging-in-Publication Data

Lawrence, of the Resurrection, Brother, 1611-1691.
  [Pratique de la présence de Dieu. Selections]
  The practice of the presence of God / Brother Lawrence; edited
and paraphrased by Donald E. Demaray.
        p.   cm.
    ISBN 0-8189-0770-3
    1. Christian life — Catholic authors.   I. Demaray, Donald E.
II. Title.
BX2349.L3825   1997
248.4'82 — dc21   96-53201
                                                         CIP

Produced and designed in the United States of America by the
Fathers and Brothers of the Society of St. Paul,
2187 Victory Boulevard, Staten Island, New York 10314,
as part of their communications apostolate.

ISBN: 0-8189-0770-3

Printing Information:

Current Printing - first digit   1   2   3   4   5   6   7   8   9   10

Year of Current Printing - first year shown

1997   1998   1999   2000   2001   2002   2003   2004   2005

Contents

Preface

We know little of the seventeenth-century saint most frequently called Brother Lawrence. Born in 1611 in the part of France called Lorraine, his parents gave him the name Nicholas Herman. He grew up to become a soldier and a servant waiting tables. He had no formal education, but became a Brother in his mid-fifties at a Carmelite monastery in Paris. There he labored in the kitchen, calling himself a servant, and remained until his death at age eighty (1691).

In the monastery his fellow brothers saw him as a simple and serene person of sound faith. Even in the kitchen, amid the clang and clatter of the pots and pans, he lived in God's presence, and so consistently that whether at work or at the Lord's Table, he sensed God in the same degree.

He became a legend in France; people inquired about how anyone could live with such peace and reality. No wonder, then, that the year 1692, shortly after his death, saw some of his correspondence made public. The letters, written in Brother Lawrence's own hand, document his sources of peace. He knew the *shalom* of God does not originate in the glitter of the world, nor in the deceptiveness of things.

In the seventeenth century, people sensed the authenticity of his faith. "For the past forty years our brother has hardly ever turned from the Presence of God" (from the original Preface by a monastery brother, 1692).

Long considered one of the Christian classics, *The Practice of the Presence of God*, like other ancient documents, needs updating in today's language. Why rob readers in our own time of such a gold mine? Why not put nuggets within reach?

That explains what I have tried to do in this rendering housed in contemporary format. My fervent prayer is that by these twin vehicles, language and form, today's seekers will find truth at once ready and vivid.

Brother Lawrence's abbott, Joseph de Beaufort, collected notes and letters, and put them into a book. My selections come from that book. One will look long and far for a record of comparable simplicity and joy resulting from living in the Presence of God.

Donald E. Demaray
Professor of Speech and Preaching
Asbury Theological Seminary
Wilmore, Kentucky

Pentecost Season

THE PRACTICE OF THE PRESENCE OF GOD

PART ONE

Conversations

The First Conversation

AUGUST 3, 1666

The very first time I saw Brother Lawrence?
   August 3, 1666.
He told me God had treated him
   most especially well:
      Brother Lawrence had come to conversion
         at age 18.
   His conversion took place like this:
      In the winter he saw a tree
         stripped of its leaves.
            "Before long, the leaves will return,"
               he thought to himself.
            "Renewed, the tree will produce
               flowers and fruit too."
      His meditations continued:
         "*God* causes all this!"

Well! he never recovered from this fresh awareness.
   Somehow, with that bursting revelation
      of God and His works,
         heaven cut him loose from the world,

                    fire ignited inside him —
                          fire that made him love God,
                          fire that has burned brightly
                          and consistently,
                          for forty years.

Brother Lawrence said he was
    a foot messenger for a Mr. Fieubert,
        treasurer of the monastery.
Brother Lawrence characterized himself as
    a big awkward fellow,
        always breaking things.
He asked for permanent residence in the monastery,
    thinking that in this setting
        God would punish him for his awkwardness,
            and his other faults too.
But God surprised him!
    Only happiness came to him
        in the monastery.

Brother Lawrence went on to say
    we should establish ourselves
        in God
            so that we sense His presence.
How do we do that?
    By having frequent conversations
        with God.

What a downright shame, he said,
to cut off conversations
with God!
When we stop listening to God,
shifting attention to
trifles and monkey-business,
how shameful indeed!

More, we should feed and nourish
our souls with
high and noble thoughts of God.
Those elevated thoughts will
yield great joy because
increased devotion does that.
We ought to put a fire
under our faith.
We do not need to have
so little faith (pity!).
People tend to
divert their attentions
away from faith,
amusing themselves with
trivial devotions,
devotions without the daily stability of faith.
Faith is stable,
stable as can be.
Faith is the way of the Church.

Good! because faith can make us
truly happy,
genuinely fulfilled in God.

Really, we must give ourselves
completely to God,
both physically
and
spiritually,
seeking fulfillment only in doing
His will.
His will may lead us
through some pretty rough experiences or
through some pretty nice experiences.
Whichever,
God uses both kinds of experiences;
the surrendered person senses that.

Actually,
we must stand faithful in
dry times
when we do not feel Him near,
when prayer becomes irksome.
You see, God tests our love
for Him
when prayer seems bothersome.
Dry times? An opportunity for genuine surrender.

Surrender under such conditions
  promotes spiritual formation.

Brother Lawrence went on:
  the miseries and sins of the world
      (one hears about them daily)
    really did not surprise him.
  Rather, he showed surprise that more
    bad things did not happen,
      since malignant sinners can
        spread a lot of disease.
  For his part,
    Brother Lawrence prayed for sinners.
  Knowing full well that
    God could remedy the bad things,
      he lost no sleep over
        the evil in the world.

To arrive at that level of resignation,
  which God requires,
    keep an eagle eye out for
      your passions
        which mingle with spiritual experiences,
      as well as those heavy passions
        we associate with gross evil.
  God, you know, throws light on
    those emotions

for those who really want to
serve Him.

Brother Lawrence said that if I
really wanted to serve like that,
I could come to him
as often as I wanted
with no fear that I would
trouble him.
But he added firmly that
if I did not come with sincere intention,
I should not visit him again.

The Second Conversation

Brother Lawrence began this session saying
　　love had always governed him —
　　　　real love that has no
　　　　　　selfish objective.
He had resolved to make loving God
　　the purpose of everything he did.
This way of relating to God brought
　　full satisfaction.
　　　　Even picking up straw
　　　　　　gladdened his heart,
　　　　　　　　for reaching down to the ground
　　　　　　　　　　to get the straw,
　　　　　　　　　　if done to show love to God,
　　　　　　　　　　　made him happy.
　　　　The clue? loving God and nothing else,
　　　　　　not even God's gifts.

Brother Lawrence said that for a long time
　　he suffered deeply
　　　　due to his belief that he would die

damned.
Nobody in the world could have
 changed his mind.
But he worked through this false belief
 this way:
  "I took up the religious life
   only to love God,
  and I endeavored to do
   everything just for Him.
Whatever becomes of me,
  lost or saved,
I have resolved always to do
  everything
   purely out of love for God.
By the time I die,
 I will have done everything I
  possibly could to love
   God."

Brother Lawrence had suffered
 a troubled mind over thoughts of
  damnation
   for four years!
 He had suffered a great deal.
But at last! he saw that his
 troubles issued from his
  lack of faith.

Since *that* discovery
   perfect freedom and abundant
      joy lived in him.
   He had placed his sins
      between himself and God
         (so to speak),
      to tell God he certainly did not
         deserve His favors.
   But what a beautiful reality!
God showered him
   with all kinds of favors
      in abundance.

Brother Lawrence told how to form the
   habit
      of talking with God all the time,
         referring all we do to
            Him.
   The secret:
   Ask God in a spirit of genuine diligence.
         After a little care and
         after a little time,
            we will discover that His love
            excites us to continual
               conversation with God
               with no difficulty.
He said he expected,

after the pleasant days God had given him,
that he would have his turn
at pain and suffering.
But this did not make him uneasy.
After all, he had no control over that,
and, besides, God would not fail
to give him strength
to bear it.

When an opportunity presented itself
to do something nice for someone,
Brother Lawrence talked to God
like this:
"Lord, I cannot do this
unless you help me."
The answer always came —
more than enough help!
When Brother Lawrence failed
at his work or duty,
he calmly confessed his fault
like this:
"Dear God,
I shall never do better
if you leave me to myself;
You only can keep me
from falling;
You alone can mend

what I have broken."
After such a prayer
he allowed himself no uneasiness.
He believed we ought to act
with God
in the greatest simplicity,
talking to Him
frankly
and
plainly,
and fervently asking
His help
in all we do,
and right while we're
doing what we do.
"God," said Brother Lawrence,
"never fails to come through" —
that he knew from
everyday experience.

Another beautiful insight came in
recounting his recent trip to
Burgundy
to buy the wine provisions for the
monastery.
He did not welcome this task
because

He did not have a business head,
He suffered a limp,
He could not walk normally
   on board the wine boat
      — he had to roll himself over the casks.
But none of these hang-ups
   gave him fits
      —not even the purchasing.
He told God He had sent him
   on this assignment.
After the whole transaction came to an end,
   he looked back and saw the
      business nicely done.
The year before
   he had a similar assignment in the town of
      Auvergne.
At that time, too, he did not feel
   he had much of a business head;
      in fact, he could not follow the
         transaction very closely,
      but the whole thing came out
         very well.

Likewise, with his business in the
   kitchen
      — by nature he could not work on the wavelength
         of his job —

so he just got used to doing
  everything
    for the love of God.
No matter what he did
  he prayed
    for God's grace to do his
      assignment.
Just there lies the secret of finding
  every task easy
    — and that over a period of fifteen years!
      He found himself very well pleased with
        his job,
          even though prepared to quit
            the task
          as he had easily quit his earlier
            assignment.
His reasoning?
  In every situation he thoroughly
    enjoyed doing little tasks for
      God.

Actually, for Brother Lawrence,
  the set times for prayer
    seemed to him no different than
      other times.
He did, of course, retire to
    pray

at the times set by his
     superior,
but he did not ask for
  these special times,
nor particularly want them,
   because his busiest and biggest work
    did not divert him from
      God.
He knew fully his call to
  love God
    in everything he did,
     and this he tried to do
      faithfully.
But in this he needed no spiritual director
   to advise him;
  He did need a confessor to assure him of
   sins forgiven.
He knew his faults very well
  but did not permit himself
   discouragement over them.
He confessed his sins,
  never asking God to excuse them;
   then went right on
    loving and adoring God
     and with peace in his heart.

This good man consulted nobody
    when a problem weighed on his mind.
        He knew completely,
            by the light of faith,
                that God stood by him.
He contented himself by
    focusing all his actions on
        God
    — that is, by doing absolutely everything
        to please God,
            no matter what would happen.
He learned, you see, that
    useless thoughts
        spoil everything.
Exactly there! at the point of
    useless thoughts,
        mischief begins.
The clue?
    Reject all useless thoughts.
    Reject them the moment they
        rear their ugly heads, and show
            their useless impertinence.
After all, they could clobber
        your salvation.
    Reject them all and return to
        inner communion with God.

When Brother Lawrence began
   to learn constant
      communion with God,
         he often spent his prayer period
            rejecting wandering thoughts,
         only to find himself
            caught up in distractions.
He just couldn't regulate
   his devotions by the methods
      some succeed at.
Nonetheless he had given
   forced meditation a try,
      but finally gave it up as a bad job.
         He had no explanation for this.

He learned, too, that all
   bodily mortifications,
      as well as other exercises,
         come to no good
      unless they actually serve
         to bring us close to God
            in love.
He had given careful thought to
   the devices for getting to God,
      but learned the quickest way
         to get there meant
            going straight to God.

How?
By continually loving God
— he called this "a continual exercise
of love" —
and by doing everything for
His sake.

Brother Lawrence said we ought
to make a great distinction
between the acts of
intellect
and
will.
He believed the intellect
of comparatively little value,
and the will
of supreme value.
Our only business, he said,
is to love God
and to delight ourselves in Him.
All kinds of disciplines,
no matter how rugged,
prove quite useless
if not motivated by love of God.
Disciplines do not remove sin!
Without anxiety,
we should expect

                pardon
                        for our sins
                                by Jesus' blood.
Our business, then?
        Just loving God with
                all our hearts.
Amazing! God seems to have
        given the greatest favors
                to the
                        greatest sinners.
                                What monuments to His mercy!
He noticed that the
        greatest pains and pleasures in this world
                do not compare with
                        the pains and pleasures experienced
                                in the spiritual world.
This explains why Brother Lawrence got uptight
        about nothing;
                Nor did he fear anything.
        He had but one goal:
                not to offend God.
        He suffered no qualms
                because, as he said,
                        "When I fail in duty,
                                I acknowledge my error immediately,
                                admitting I often make mistakes,
                                and cannot improve if left to myself.

When I do not fail,
    I give thanks,
        acknowledging that the
            strength comes from Him."

The Third Conversation

Brother Lawrence said that the
   foundation
      of his spiritual life lay in
        a high view of God,
        a high respect for God
        — this by faith.
Once he got this firmly
   rooted and grounded in himself
     he had no care
   except to
     reject all thoughts
       contrary to a high view of God
       in order to do everything
        to show his love for God.
When sometimes he had not
   thought of God
     for quite some time,
      he did not allow himself
      to get upset;
But after acknowledging his
   wretchedness before God,

he returned to Him
with much greater
trust.
Something about forgetting
Him
stimulated remembering
Him.
This, too, he found true
in the fresh discovery of
God:
The trust we put in
God
honors Him very much
and draws great help right down to
us.

Brother Lawrence learned
something else:
God cannot deceive us,
and He will not allow
a perfectly surrendered soul
— a soul determined
to suffer anything for His sake —
to suffer long.
He said that he had so often
experienced the quick help of
divine grace

on all kinds of occasions,
   that on the basis of such experiences,
      he did not get uptight
         about business before time to do it.
But when the time came to do it,
   he found in God
      (as in a clear mirror)
         just what he needed to do.
In fact, only lately
   he had acted like this,
      anticipating no care or hang-up.
This way of coping
   had now become
      habitual,
   but early on, before he had learned
      this lesson on trust,
         his heart filled with
            care and anxiety
               when he went to do business.

Marvelously relaxed,
   he gave no attention to what he
      had done once
         — the past is past —
   and certainly gave no anxious concern
      to his activities while doing them.
Leaving the eating table,

he could not tell you what he ate.
But this he knew:
   Whatever he did,
     he did with a single view —
      to love God,
        giving thanks to Him for
          directing his acts.
   He also thanked God for
     his ability to identify with others.
   Everything he did
     he did very simply,
      in the style which kept him
        steadfastly in *the*
          loving presence of God.

When business diverted him a little
   from the thought of God,
     God sent a fresh remembrance of Himself,
      and so fired and excited Brother Lawrence
      that he could hardly contain himself.
But usually Brother Lawrence
   saw himself more united to God
     during business activities than
      when he went off by himself
        to get quiet for his devotions.
Retirement seemed to
   bring much dryness of spirit.

He expected that some time he would
  suffer greatly in body and mind.
The worst thing that could happen to him
  would be the loss of the sense of God,
    which he had enjoyed for so long.
But the goodness of God
  gave him ample reason
    to believe God would not forsake him completely.
More, God would give him
  strength
    to bear whatever evil He
      permitted to happen to him.
Therefore he feared nothing
  and had no reason to consult
    anybody about his thoughts.
Whenever he had attempted
  to talk to somebody about his problems,
    he always came away
      more perplexed.
More, he knew in himself
  his readiness to lay down his life
    for the love of God,
      and so had no apprehension of danger.
That perfect resignation
  to God
    was the sure way to heaven.
      A way which always

provided enough
light
for our conduct.

At the beginning of the
spiritual life,
we must show faithfulness in
doing our duty
and
denying ourselves.
Well, after our personal disciplines
establish
themselves in our lives,
unspeakable pleasures follow!
And what about difficulties?
You have Jesus Christ
to help you
— beg His help and grace.
With Him everything becomes
easy.
Do you know why many do not
advance
in the Christian life?
They put their personal disciplines,
such as penances and special exercises,
over the love of God.

But what's the real purpose of
    devotion?
One's true motivations and behavior patterns
        define the character of one's work —
            everyone sees that!
Just here we see the fly in the ointment
    and this explains why we see so little
        solid good done.
Actually, we need neither
    art nor science
        for going to God.
All we need?
    A heart for going to God
        resolutely determined
            to apply itself to
                nothing but Him —
                    just for His sake,
                    just for love of Him.

The Fourth Conversation

NOVEMBER 25, 1667

Brother Lawrence talked with me fervently,
   and with great openness of heart
     about his way of
      going to God.
   (Some of this he had already touched on.)
The bottom line?
   Our wholehearted renunciation
     of anything we know about
      that does not lead to God.

He said we could
   accustom
     ourselves to a continual
      conversation
       with Him,
     — and that with
      freedom
      and
      simplicity.
We need only recognize
   God

intimately present with us,
　　and address Him every moment.
This will help us
　secure His help
　　for knowing His will in
　　　uncertain matters,
　　and for doing those things
　　　we know He plainly requires
　　　　of us.
He will help us give them to
　　God
　before we do them,
　　and then to give Him thanks
　when we have finished
　　doing them.

In our continual conversation with
　　God
　we really
　　praise,
　　adore and
　　love Him
　　　incessantly
　because of His infinite goodness
　　and perfection.
We must never get discouraged ~~Not Easy~~
　because of our sins;

We should pray for His grace
  with perfect confidence,
    relying on the infinite merits of our
      Lord.
God never fails to offer us
  His grace
    in every activity.
  He perceives our need
    very clearly,
      and never fails to provide help,
    unless, said Brother Lawrence,
      one wanders from *a sense of*
        God's presence or
        forgets to ask His help.

God never fails to throw
  light
    on our doubts
      when we have no other design
        than to please Him.
Our sanctification
  does not depend on changing the way
    we do things,
      but doing for God *Little Things*
  what we normally do for ourselves.
How sad to see many people
  mistake the means for the end,

addicting themselves to certain works,
  which they do very imperfectly
because of their human or selfish
  motivations!

The finest way Brother Lawrence
  found for going to God
    related simply to doing his
      daily business
    with no view to pleasing people
      (Gal 1:10; Eph 6:5-6).
  And, so far as possible,
    just for the love of God.
What a delusion to think
  the times of prayer
    ought to differ from
      other times!
God strictly obliges us to stay
  as close to Him
    by action in the time of action
      as
    by prayer in the season of prayer. *forever*

Brother Lawrence defined his perspective on prayer:
  The sense of the presence of God,
    his soul aware of nothing but
      God's love.

When appointed times of prayer
    came and went,
        he found no difference
            because he went right on
                with God,
                    praising and
                    blessing Him
                        with all his might,
                    so that he lived his life with
                    continual joy.
Yet he hoped God would give
    some suffering
        so he could grow stronger.
We ought, once for all,
    to put our whole trust in God;
        and we should do so heartily,
            making a total surrender of
            ourselves to Him,
                secure in the knowledge that
                God will never deceive us.

Again, we ought never weary of
    doing little things
        for the love of God,
    Who really doesn't think about
        the greatness of what we do,
        but the love with which we do it.

If at first we often fail
    to do everything for the
        love of God,
            never mind;
The new habit will form in us
    in time.
Once fixed,
    the habit naturally produces its acts
        without care and to our great delight.

The whole substance of religion?
    Faith,
    Hope,
    Love;
        The practice of these three defines
            The Way
                we unite to God's will.
        All else we must use
            only as a means to arrive at our goal,
                and even the means get
                    swallowed up by
                        Faith,
                        Hope,
                        Love.

All things are possible to the one
    who believes;

They are less difficult to the one
  who hopes;
They are still easier to the one
  who loves;
They are even easier to the one
  who practices all three virtues.
What should we set as the
  ultimate goal
    in this life?
The answer:
  The most perfect
    worshippers of God
      we can possibly be,
        like we hope for ourselves
          throughout eternity.
When we begin the spiritual life
  we should consider and examine
    to the bottom of our being
      what we are.
We will find ourselves
  worthy of contempt
    and surely not deserving of the name
      Christian.
We will find ourselves subject to
  all kinds of misery and accidents
    to trouble us and play havoc with our health.
Our body chemistry can get upset,

our inward moods and
external expressions can be miserable.
In a word, we are persons
God can humble
by many pains and lots of hard work
inside and outside.
Knowing all this, we should not show surprise
when people
trouble,
tempt,
oppose,
contradict us.
We ought, on the contrary to
accept these troubles,
temptations,
contradictions,
and bear them so long as
God pleases,
knowing they come as highly
advantageous to us.
The greater the perfection one desires,
the greater the dependence on divine grace.

PART TWO

Letters

The First Letter

Dear Friend:

I write because you want to hear from me
  so badly
    about how I arrived at the
      habitual sense of God's presence.
       This *sense* is God's gift,
But I write with great difficulty
  and only because you insist.
    Moreover, I write
      only under the condition that you
       show this letter to no one.
If I knew you would let others see it,
  all the desire I have
    for your spiritual formation
      would leave me powerless to make me write.

Now to answering your question:
  I found many books that give
    lots of ways to come to God.
  They suggest any number of

spiritual exercises.
But I concluded that the books would
  puzzle me
    more than help me.
After all,
  I sought for no more than
    how to be God's
    and God's alone.
My goal made me
  resolve
    to give my all for *The All.*
So, after giving myself wholly to
  God,
    to take care of my sins,
      I renounced —
        because I loved Him so much —
      everything not of God.
Now I began to live
  as if He and I were the only ones
    alive in the world.
Sometimes I thought of myself as
  a poor criminal, and
    He as my Judge.
At other times,
  I thought of Him as my Father.
Always I worshipped Him as often as I could,
  keeping my mind in His holy presence.

When I wandered
  I brought Him back to my mind.
This was a painful exercise
  but I persisted,
    even through all difficulties.
But never did I trouble or
  disquiet my mind
    when my thoughts wandered involuntarily.
I made practicing His presence
  my business
    as much right through
      the day
        as at the appointed times of prayer.
At all times —
  every hour,
  every minute,
  even at the height of business —
    I drove away from my mind
      everything interrupting the
        sense of the presence of God.

That, in a nutshell, gives you
  my everyday practice
    ever since I took up religion in earnest.
Though I have practiced His presence
  very imperfectly,
    I have greatly benefited from

what I have done.
The benefits, I know very well, all come
    from God
        — His mercy and goodness —
            because we can do nothing without Him,
                and I can do fewer good things
                    than anyone!

But when we stand firm
    to keep ourselves in His holy presence
        and to make Him absolutely
            central in our lives;
This not only hinders us from
    offending Him
        or doing anything that displeases Him
            (at least willfully),
        it also gives rise to freedom
            — a divine freedom —
        and, if you will not misunderstand me,
            a familiarity with God
                that makes possible
                    asking and receiving
                        the graces we need.

To summarize:
    Repeating these acts often
        translates them into habit,

then the presence of God
becomes, so to speak,
natural to us.
Please join me in giving Him thanks
for His great goodness to me;
I can never wonder enough at
the many favors
He has done for so miserable a sinner as I!
I want the whole world,
material things included,
to praise Him.
Amen.

I am, in our Lord,
Yours very truly.

The Second Letter

*M*y Dear Friend in the Ministry:

I'm not a bookish man
    (that's no hang-up with me),
  but you may love books and if so
    I would like to know
      how they enrich your life.
Sometime ago
  a person of piety
    told me that
      the spiritual life is a life of grace.
        It begins with fear like a slave suffers;
        It increases by hope of eternal life;
        It comes to fulfillment by pure love.
      Each of these states has its own stages,
        by which one finally arrives at
          spiritual fulfillment.

I myself have not followed
  such a step-by-step program.
On the contrary

— from what instincts I do not know —
    I found steps and stages
      discouraged me.
This explains why,
    when I entered religion full time
      I resolved simply to give myself to God.
How could I do better
    in return for His love?
Because I loved Him
    I renounced everything that
      didn't come from God.

For the first years
    I usually employed myself
      during the times set apart for devotion
        with thoughts of
          death,
          judgment,
          heaven,
          hell and
          my sins.
(This pattern I continued for some years.)
The rest of the day I applied my mind,
    even in the flow of business,
      to *the presence of God*.
I considered Him always *with me* and
    in me.

At length I came habitually
    to practice the presence
        during the time set apart.
When I finally saw what was
    happening,
        my heart leapt for joy!
            and comfort washed over me.
Something else —
    This practice gave me
        a view of God
            so high
                only the eyes of faith inside me
                    could even begin to
                        comprehend Him
                            with any kind of
                                satisfaction.

Well, that gives you my beginning,
    and yet I must tell you that
        for the first ten years
            I suffered a great deal.
I feared I did not
    devote myself to God
        as I wished.
Also, my past sins
    bugged me.
In contrast, I saw the great unmerited

favors God did for me.
   — These things caused
    my sufferings.
During this time
  I often fell
   but got up,
    dusted myself off,
     and went on.

Sometimes my perception said:
  Everyone stands against me,
  Reason stands against me,
  Even God stands against me.
   I held on by faith alone.
Sometimes my troubled thoughts told me that
  to believe God had given me His favors
   was all a presumption,
   that I only pretended
    I had arrived easily
     where others arrive with difficulty.
I even found temptation to believe I had
  willfully deluded myself and
   that I had no salvation at all.

I thought I would have to
  live out my life
   with these troubles.

(By the way, my troubled thoughts
    did not diminish my trust in God
    one bit;
  they only served to
    increase
      my faith.)
Well! when I thought I would
  have to live with my troubles
    all my life,
      I found myself changed all at once.
My soul now felt
  a profound inward peace
    because it had come to
      its center,
      its place of rest.
Ever since that time
  I have walked in
    God's pathway for me —
      Simply,
      In faith,
      With humility,
      With love;
  And I apply myself diligently to
    do nothing or
    think nothing
      which may displease Him.
So I hope that when I have

lived out my life
    — having done what I could —
    He will do with me
      what He pleases.

I have quit all forms of devotion
    and set times for prayer,
      except those required
        by our religious community,
          in which I play my part.
I just make my business this:
    To persevere in His holy presence.
      I stay there
        by a simple attention and
        by an absorbing passionate regard
          for God
            which I want to call
              an *actual presence of God*.
Said better,
    my soul has an
      habitual,
      silent,
      secret
      conversation with God.
        This often causes inward
          joys and raptures.
        Outwardly sometimes, too.

So much so I must
    force myself to moderate my expressions
        lest others see them.

In short, I have no doubt at all that
    my soul has lived with God
        these thirty years.
I pass over many things
    to avoid coming across as tedious,
        but I do not want to stop
            before telling you how I see myself
                relating to God,
                the one I consider my King.
I consider myself
    the most wretched of sinners,
        full of sores and corruption;
I have committed all sorts of crimes
    against the King.
Touched with a sense of regret,
    I confess to Him
        all my wickedness;
    I ask His
        forgiveness;
    I abandon myself
        into His hands
            so He can do with me
                whatever He pleases.

The King, full of mercy and goodness,
   very far from chastising me,
      Embraces me with love,
      Invites me to eat at His table,
      Serves me with His own hands,
      Gives me the key to His treasures.
   He also
      talks with me all the time
         in the most delightful way,
         in a thousand ways,
      and treats me in all respects
         as His favorite.
Now you get an idea of how,
   when I think about it,
      I see my relationship to God.
My most useful way of
   relating to God
      is this simple attention
      and real desire
         for God.
Often I find myself
   attached to God
      with greater delight than
         a baby at mother's breast,
      so that — if I dared use the expression —
         I would call this closeness to God
            suckling at the bosom of God,

because of the inexpressible
sweetness I taste
and experience there.

If sometimes my thoughts
wander from
the presence of God,
due to some necessary interruption or
due to my own human weakness,
before long, charming and delicious
thoughts too private to mention
call me back to Him.
Please reflect on my wretchedness
— I already told you about all that —
not on the great favors
God does for me,
unworthy and ungrateful as I am.

As for my regular devotional periods,
they come and go with a continuation of
the same presence of God.
Sometimes I think of myself as
a stone before a carver
about to make a statue.
Presenting myself in this way
before God,
I want Him to form

His perfect image in my soul,
to make me entirely like Himself!
At other times,
when I apply myself to prayer,
I feel my whole spirit and soul
lift right up with
no effort on my part,
and I stay there
suspended and firmly fixed in God
as its center and place of rest.

I know some charge this as
inactivity,
delusion,
self-love.
For me this is
holy activity.
It would be self-love
if the soul found itself capable of it.
While the soul absorbs itself in divine repose,
it cannot get disturbed as it did formerly
— its former habit: thoughts of self-love to
give it security —
but such thoughts now hinder rather than
help.

I cannot entertain the thought that
   the presence of God
     is mere delusion.
Why?
   The soul that enjoys God
     desires, in that experience,
       nothing but Him.
   If deluded,
     God must cure me!
       Let Him do what He pleases with me:
         I desire only Him;
         I desire only 100% devotion to Him.
Feel free, however, to let me have your opinion,
   to which I always pay close attention
     because I respect your piety.

       I am, in our Lord,
       Your friend.

The Third Letter

Dear Friend:

We have a God
   infinitely gracious,
     who knows all about our wants.
I always thought
   He would reduce you to
     your limits.
The truth is,
   He will come
     in His own time,
       and when you least expect Him.
So hope in Him more than ever;
   thank Him for the favors
     He gives you
       (I will join you in thanks);
   Thank Him particularly for the
     fortitude and patience
       He gives you in your
         troubles.
Just here you can see

plainly
     the care He gives you.
Comfort yourself, then, with Him,
     and give thanks for everything.

I admire the fortitude of
     Mr. de ———————.
God has given him
     a good disposition,
          and a spirit of good will.
However, a little bit of the world
     still lives in him,
          also a lot of youth.
I hope the affliction
     God sent him
          will prove wholesome medicine
               and make him take a good look
                    at himself.
What's happened to him
     should make him put
          trust in God
               Who goes with him everywhere.
Hopefully he will think of God
     as often as he can,
          especially in the greatest dangers.
               A little lifting up of the heart
                    will do the job.

A little remembrance of God
— a single act of inward worship
even though one is on the march
with sword in hand —
means prayers, however short, become
very acceptable to God.
Far from lessening
a soldier's courage in danger,
prayers will fortify him.

Let him think of God, then,
as much as he can.
Let him accustom himself
by degrees
to this small but holy exercise.
No one will notice it,
and nothing comes easier
than to repeat often in the day
these little interval adorations.

Recommend to him, if you will,
that he think of God
all he can
in the way I suggest
in this letter.
Such exercise makes a soldier
spiritually fit

for daily exposure to
life's dangers and salvation.
My hope and prayer is that
God will assist him
and all his family,
each of whom I would gladly help
because I am
theirs and
yours. ...

The Fourth Letter

Dear Friend:

I take this opportunity
   to communicate
      to you
         the deep feelings
            of a member of our
               religious society
            about the good things
            and continued help
               he gets from *the presence of God.*
You and I can both profit
   by having a look at the
      benefits.

You must know his
   continuous concern
      over the forty years he has spent
         in this religious congregation:
Always to live in God and
   to do nothing to displease Him.

He has but one aim:
  to love Him with a pure heart
    (though He deserves infinitely more).
He has by now so accustomed himself
  to *the divine presence*
    that he receives from Him
      non-stop help
      on all occasions.
For about thirty years his soul
  has overflowed with joys
    so continuous and
      sometimes so heavenly
  he must force himself
    to moderate them,
      preventing outward expression.

If sometimes he engages himself
  rather too much in business
    so that he absents himself from the
      divine presence,
God soon makes Himself
  felt in his soul
    and this helps him
      to focus on God
      once more.
He responds completely to
  inward promptings,

either by elevating his heart to God,
or by a quiet but genuine and fond
regard for Him,
or by the words love forms.
An example of the latter:
My God, here I am,
totally devoted to You.
Lord, shape me after
the pattern of Yourself.
Then he senses with clear feeling
that this God of love,
satisfied with such a few words,
reposes again and rests in the
very heart and center
of his soul.

You can imagine how
such experiences
give him assurance of God —
God always in the heart,
in the depths of his soul.
Such assurance
makes him incapable
of doubting God's presence
for any reason at all.

Judge for yourself
  what contentment and satisfaction
    he enjoys,
      feeling continually inside him
        so great a treasure.
He no longer anxiously
  searches for the treasure;
he has it open before him
  and may take from it
    what he pleases.
Often he complains about how blind
  the rest of us are,
    and often cries that we must be pitied
      because we content ourselves with
        so little.
God, he says,
  offers us a treasure like
    the infinite ocean,
      but we satisfy ourselves with
        a little wave of feeling,
          passing with the moment.
Our blindness hinders
    God
  and stops the currents of His graces.
But when He finds a soul
  permeated with living faith,
    He pours into it His

graces and favors
to overflowing.
There, in the soul,
they flow like a torrent,
which, when forcibly stopped
against its ordinary course,
finds its channel, then
spreads itself with
impetuosity
and
abundance.

Yes, we often stop
    this torrent
        by the little value we give it!
But let us stop it no more;
    Let us get hold of ourselves and
        break down the barrier
            which hinders the flow.
Let us make way for grace;
    let us prepare ourselves well
        because we die only once, and
            miscarriage then is irretrievable.

I say again,
    let us examine ourselves.
Time presses us and

we have no room for delay;
    our souls are at stake.
You, I believe,
    have taken effective measures
      so surprise will not attack you.
I commend you for this;
    You have done the one thing
      needed.
All of us must nevertheless always work at it,
    because not to advance in
      the spiritual life
        means
        to
      go
backwards.
But those who know their spirits
    stirred by the breath of the Holy Spirit
      go
        forward
          even
            in
              sleep.
If the ship of our soul
    tosses in wind and storm
      let us awake our Lord,
        asleep in the bottom of the boat,
          and He will quickly

               calm
                  the
                     sea.

I have taken the liberty to
   share these good thoughts
      so you can compare them with
         your own.
They will serve to
   rekindle and inflame
      your own spiritual gifts
         lest by some misfortune
            (God forbid — what a great misfortune!)
            they should cool even a little.

Let us both, then,
   recall our first blessings.
Let us profit by the
   example and experience
      of this brother,
         little known in the world,
            but known by God,
               and caressed immeasurably
                  by God.
I will pray for you;
   do pray often for me.

                     Yours in the Lord.…
                     June 1, 1682.